First Step Math

Numbers

For a free color catalog describing Gareth Stevens' list of high-quality books, call 1-800-542-2595 (USA) or 1-800-461-9120 (Canada). Gareth Stevens' Fax: (414) 225-0377.

Library of Congress Cataloging-in-Publication Data

Griffiths, Rose.
    Numbers/by Rose Griffiths; photographs by Peter Millard.
      p. cm. -- (First step math)
    Includes bibliographical references and index.
    ISBN 0-8368-1112-7
    1. Numbers, Cardinal--Juvenile literature. [1. Numerals.]
  I. Millard, Peter, ill. II. Title. III. Series.
  QA248.G75   1994
  513--dc20   94-7983

This edition first published in 1994 by
Gareth Stevens Publishing
1555 North RiverCenter Drive, Suite 201
Milwaukee, Wisconsin 53212, USA

This edition © 1994 by Gareth Stevens, Inc. Original edition published in 1993 by A&C Black (Publishers) Ltd., 35 Bedford Row, London WC1R 4JH. © 1993 A&C Black (Publishers) Ltd. Additional end matter © 1994 by Gareth Stevens, Inc.

Series editor: Patricia Lantier-Sampon
Editorial assistants: Mary Dykstra, Diane Laska
Mathematics consultant: Mike Spooner

Printed in the United States of America
1 2 3 4 5 6 7 8 9 99 98 97 96 95 94

At this time, Gareth Stevens, Inc., does not use 100 percent recycled paper, although the paper used in our books does contain about 30 percent recycled fiber. This decision was made after a careful study of current recycling procedures revealed their dubious environmental benefits. We will continue to explore recycling options.

Numbers

by Rose Griffiths
photographs by Peter Millard

Gareth Stevens Publishing
MILWAUKEE

j513
GRI

How many numbers have you seen today?

I've got numbers on my clothes.

5

The number on my badge
tells you how old I am.

How old will
I be on my
next birthday?

Can you find your age here?

Shaun is cutting
some numbers for
crayon rubbing.

2

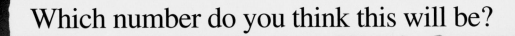

Which number do you think this will be?

Do you know which are letters and which are numbers?

We use ten different numerals.

Why do you think there are ten?

We put numerals
together to make
bigger numbers.

Some languages use other numerals.

Gujarati numerals look like this.

૦	૧	૨	૩	૪	૫	૬	૭	૮	૯
0	1	2	3	4	5	6	7	8	9

These are Roman numerals.

Can you find the number seven?

Amy has a digital alarm clock.

Where else have you seen
numerals like these?

We can write a
numeral in many
different ways.

We use numbers when we count things.

We also use numbers
when we weigh things . . .

18

and measure how
long they are.

Numbers help us tell
one thing from another.

My boat came first!

Some numbers help us find places.
I'm sending a letter to my friend.

Here's her front door.

FOR MORE INFORMATION

Notes for Parents and Teachers

As you share this book with young readers, these notes may help you explain the mathematical principles behind the different activities.

pages 4, 5, 14, 15, 18, 19, 20, 21, 22, 23 Numbers all around us

Numbers appear on items all around us, including buses, toys, clocks, street signs, calendars, clothes, and food packaging. Numbers are symbols representing real things and abstract concepts.

pages 6, 7, 24, 25 Personal numbers

Important personal numbers to children include their age, date of birth, phone number, address, and the number of people in their family. Children are more likely to be interested in numbers that mean something to them.

pages 8, 9, 13, 14, 15, 16 The shapes of numbers

Numbers can be written or printed in many different ways. Encourage children to write numbers clearly. If, at times, they write a number backward, allow them to check the number on a ruler, a clock, or a calculator for an example to copy.

pages 10, 11, 12 Numerals, numbers, letters, and words

We use letters to make words and numerals to make numbers. Sometimes, a word can be just one letter, and a number can be just one numeral.

pages 11, 12, 13, 14
Different number systems

Most people in the world use number systems based on groupings of ten, probably because people have always used their fingers to count.

The numerals most of us use today developed from an early Hindu number system that included a zero (0). This meant that numbers of any size could be written using only the numerals 1, 2, 3, 4, 5, 6, 7, 8, and 9, plus zero (0).

The value of each numeral of a number depends on its place in relation to the other numerals. This is called place value. For example, in 1,304, the value of 3 is 300; while in 435, the value of 3 is 30. The Roman system (page 14) is built in a completely different way, without using zero. The symbols it uses include I=1, V=5, X=10, L=50, C=100, and M=1,000.

pages 6, 17-25
Using numbers

Numbers are used for counting and for measuring things, such as time, money, temperature, length, or capacity. They are also used as a code or a label to tell things apart. Some numbers may be issued in chronological order, such as when waiting in line for service. Some numbers, such as house numbers, page numbers, or map references, help us locate things.

page 11, 13, 14, 21
Cardinal and ordinal numbers

The numbers we use for counting (1, 2, 3 . . .) are called cardinal numbers. Ordinal numbers (1st, 2nd, 3rd . . .) are the ones we use when we put things in order.

Things to Do

1. Number spotting
Look for numbers on objects around you. You can write a list or draw pictures of the things you see with numbers on them. You might want to look for just one number, such as your age, and see how many different places you can find it. Or you might want to look for objects with numbers in chronological order, such as 1, then 2, then 3, and so forth. What is the largest number you can find? Which numbers do you see most often?

2. Make a number line
Cut large, colorful numbers out of magazine advertisements. Put the numbers in order to make a number line from 1 to 10. Compare the styles of the numbers. Did the artists who designed the ads use different colors and styles? Why do you think they chose these particular colors and styles?

3. Number rubbing
Draw the shape of a number on cardboard and cut it out. Put a piece of paper over the number and use a crayon to color evenly over the top until the number shows through. You can use your number rubbings to decorate a math folder for school, make a number picture, or make number patterns.

4. Food facts
Look at the numbers on food packages in your kitchen or at the supermarket. Be sure to look at all sides of the box or package. What do the numbers tell you?

Fun Facts about Numbers

1. An abacus is a counting machine made of beads strung on parallel wires attached to a rectangular frame. The abacus was invented about three thousand years ago. It is still used in some parts of the world.

2. A computer's number system is based on two, not ten. This is called a binary system.

3. It would take approximately twelve days to count to one million and thirty-two years to count to one billion, if each count is one second long.

4. Arithmetic is a type of mathematics. The two basic operations of arithmetic are addition and multiplication. The result of adding two numbers is called a sum. The result of multiplying two numbers is called a product.

5. There are over five billion people living on Earth.

6. Zip codes help postal workers sort the mail efficiently. The five-number zip code used in the United States was introduced in 1963.

7. Scientists around the world use numbered aluminum bands to learn more about birds and other animals. For example, a lightweight aluminum band is attached to a bird's leg. The number on the band is then entered into a computer that compiles information on the activities of that particular bird.

Glossary

badge — something, such as a pin or a patch, that is worn to show that someone belongs to a certain group or has won an award of some sort.

digital — showing information in changing numerals. For example, a digital clock tells time in constantly changing numerals instead of using metal or plastic hands that move around a circle of set numbers.

Gujarati — a language and number system from India.

languages — systems of words, numbers, or other symbols that people use to communicate with each other.

letters — the symbols that make up an alphabet.

measure — to find out the size or amount of something. For instance, by using a ruler and scale, you can measure how long something is or how much it weighs.

number — a word or symbol used to count things. Two (2) and twelve (12) are numbers.

numeral — a symbol or a group of symbols that represent a number. In the number thirty-five (35), three (3) and five (5) are numerals.

Roman numerals — symbols in a numbering system invented by the ancient Romans. In this system, symbols stand for numbers. For example, I=1, V=5, and X=10.

Places to Visit

Everything we do involves some basic mathematical principles. Listed below are a few museums that offer a wide variety of mathematical information and experiences. You may also be able to locate other museums in your area. Just remember: you don't always have to visit a museum to experience the wonders of mathematics. Math is everywhere!

The Smithsonian Institution
1000 Jefferson Drive SW
Washington, D.C. 20560

The Exploratorium
3601 Lyon Street
San Francisco, CA 94123

Royal British Columbia Museum
675 Belleville Street
Victoria, British Columbia
V8V 1X4

Ontario Science Center
770 Don Mills Road
Don Mills, Ontario
M3C 1T3

Museum of Science and Industry
57th Street and Lake Shore Drive
Chicago, IL 60637

More Books to Read

Counting Kangaroos, A Book
    About Numbers
        Marcia Leonard
        (Troll Associates)

Counting on Frank
        Rod Clement
        (Gareth Stevens)

*Fish Eyes, A Book You Can
    Count On*
    Lois Ehlert
    (Harcourt Brace Jovanovich)

How Many?
    D. MacKinnon, A. Sieveking
    (Dial Books)

How Many? How Much?
    Monica Weiss
    (Troll Associates)

My First Number Book
    Marie Heinst
    (Dorling Kindersley)

Videotapes

Clifford's Fun with Numbers
    (Scholastic)

*Place Values: Ones, Tens,
    Hundreds* (Coronet)

Index